Little Mitchie

CAN A TURTLE COME OUT OF ITS SHELL?

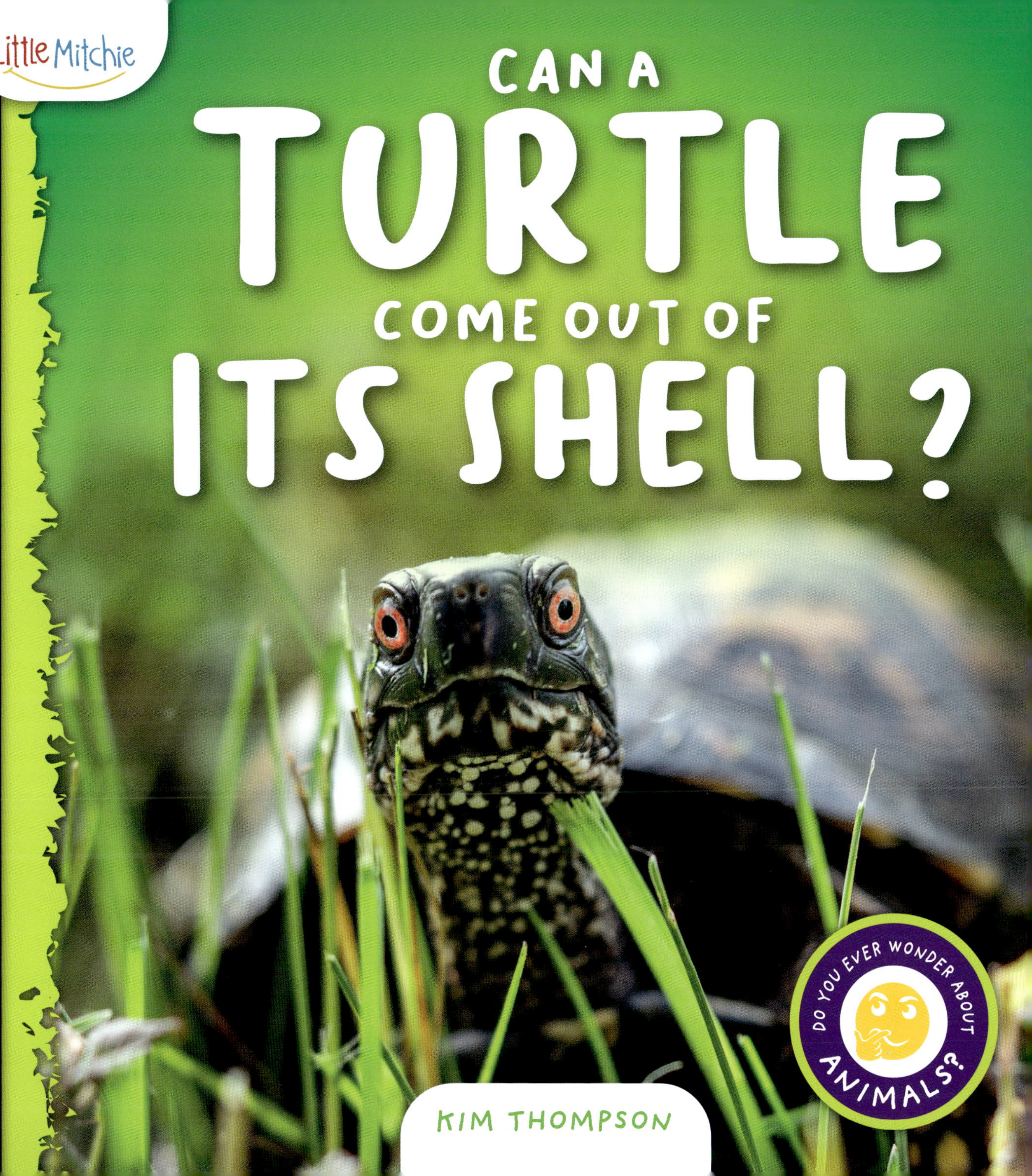

DO YOU EVER WONDER ABOUT ANIMALS?

KIM THOMPSON

CREATING YOUNG NONFICTION READERS

Little Mitchie books spark curiosity and support early nonfiction reading for students in Grades 2-3. Designed to build vocabulary, support second language learners, and prepare readers for middle-grade content, each book includes helpful tips for parents and educators to build confidence and deepen understanding of the world.

TIPS FOR READING NONFICTION WITH BEGINNING READERS

Talk about Nonfiction

Begin by explaining that nonfiction books give us information that is true. The book will be organized around a specific topic or idea, and we may learn new facts through reading.

Look at the Parts

Most nonfiction books have helpful features. Our *Little Mitchie* titles include color photographs and graphic aids, a table of contents, a glossary, and an index. Share the purpose of these features with your reader.

Color Photos and Graphic Aids

A lot of information can be found by "reading" photos, charts, maps, and other graphic aids found within nonfiction texts. Help your reader learn more about the different ways information can be displayed.

Table of Contents

Located at the front of the book, this list shows the big ideas within the text and the page numbers where they can be found.

Glossary

Located at the back of the book, the glossary defines key words and phrases that are related to the topic. These words and phrases can be found in the text in colored type.

Index

Located at the back of the book, an index is an alphabetical list of topics and the page numbers where they can be found.

With a little help and guidance about reading nonfiction, you can feel good about introducing a young reader to the world of *Little Mitchie* nonfiction books.

Little Mitchie is an imprint of:

Mitchell Lane
PUBLISHERS

2001 SW 31st Avenue
Hallandale, FL 33009
mitchelllanepub.com

First Edition, 2027.

Author: Kim Thompson
Designer: Jen Bowers

Library of Congress Cataloging-in-Publication Data
Title: Can a Turtle Come Out of Its Shell /
by Kim Thompson

Description: Hallandale, FL :
Mitchell Lane Publishers, [2027]

Identifiers:
ISBN 979-8-89260-920-3 (library bound)
ISBN 979-8-89260-975-3 (eBook)

Library of Congress Control Number: 2026936377

PHOTO CREDITS
Shutterstock: cover, p.1 ©2025 The Camera Dad, p.5 ©2009 john a. shaw, p.6–7 ©2013 Randy Bjorklund, p.9 ©2006 EcoPrint, p.10–11 ©2014 jeep2499, p.13 ©2014 Andrei Armiagov, p.14 ©2013 danz13, p.17 ©2020 Jason Schronce, p.18–19 ©2006 Elena Kouptsova -Vasic, p.20 ©2009 Christian Musat, p.21 ©2006 Nikita Tiunov, p.22 ©Alexander_P

TABLE OF CONTENTS

Chapter One

QUESTIONS

Have you ever watched a turtle or a **tortoise**? Could you see its head and limbs, or were they tucked inside the shell?

You probably wondered about the **reptile**. You may have asked these questions.

1. What is a turtle shell?
2. Why does a turtle have a shell?
3. Can a turtle come all the way out of its shell?

Chapter Two

A DOME OF BONE

A turtle shell is made of bone. It is very hard. The dome-shaped top is the **carapace**. The bottom is the **plastron**.

ANIMAL WONDER

Shells can be black, green, brown, yellow, red, or orange. They have spots, stripes, and other patterns.

The top and bottom join at the sides. They form one solid structure.

The shell is covered with hard plates called **scutes**. Sometimes, scutes shed. New ones grow in their place.

ANIMAL WONDER

Scutes are made of **keratin**. This is the same substance that makes up your fingernails.

Chapter Three

ARMOR

A shell helps a turtle stay healthy. It protects the animal's soft **organs**. It keeps germs out.

ANIMAL WONDER

The shell is **buoyant**. It helps the turtle move easily through water.

Most turtles can **retract** their heads, legs, and tails inside their shells. The shell is like armor. It protects the animal from threats. When danger comes, **predators** can't take a bite.

Chapter Four

NOT A HOUSE

The bone that forms a turtle's shell is alive. It is part of the animal's skeleton. The scutes are like skin. They can feel.

The shell grows with the animal. A turtle can't get too big for its shell.

Shells can't be removed or replaced. Without a shell, a turtle would die.

ANIMAL WONDER

Turtles are some of the oldest animals. They lived with dinosaurs!

Chapter Five

ANSWERS

Now, you can answer your questions.

1. WHAT IS A TURTLE SHELL?

It is a one-piece structure made of bone and covered with hard plates called scutes.

2. WHY DOES A TURTLE HAVE A SHELL?

The shell protects a turtle from predators, diseases, and other threats.

3. CAN A TURTLE COME ALL THE WAY OUT OF ITS SHELL?

No. A shell may look like a house, but it is part of the animal's body.

ANIMAL WONDER

Keep asking questions about animals. That's how you learn about the amazing creatures that share our world!

TURTLE SHELL DIAGRAM

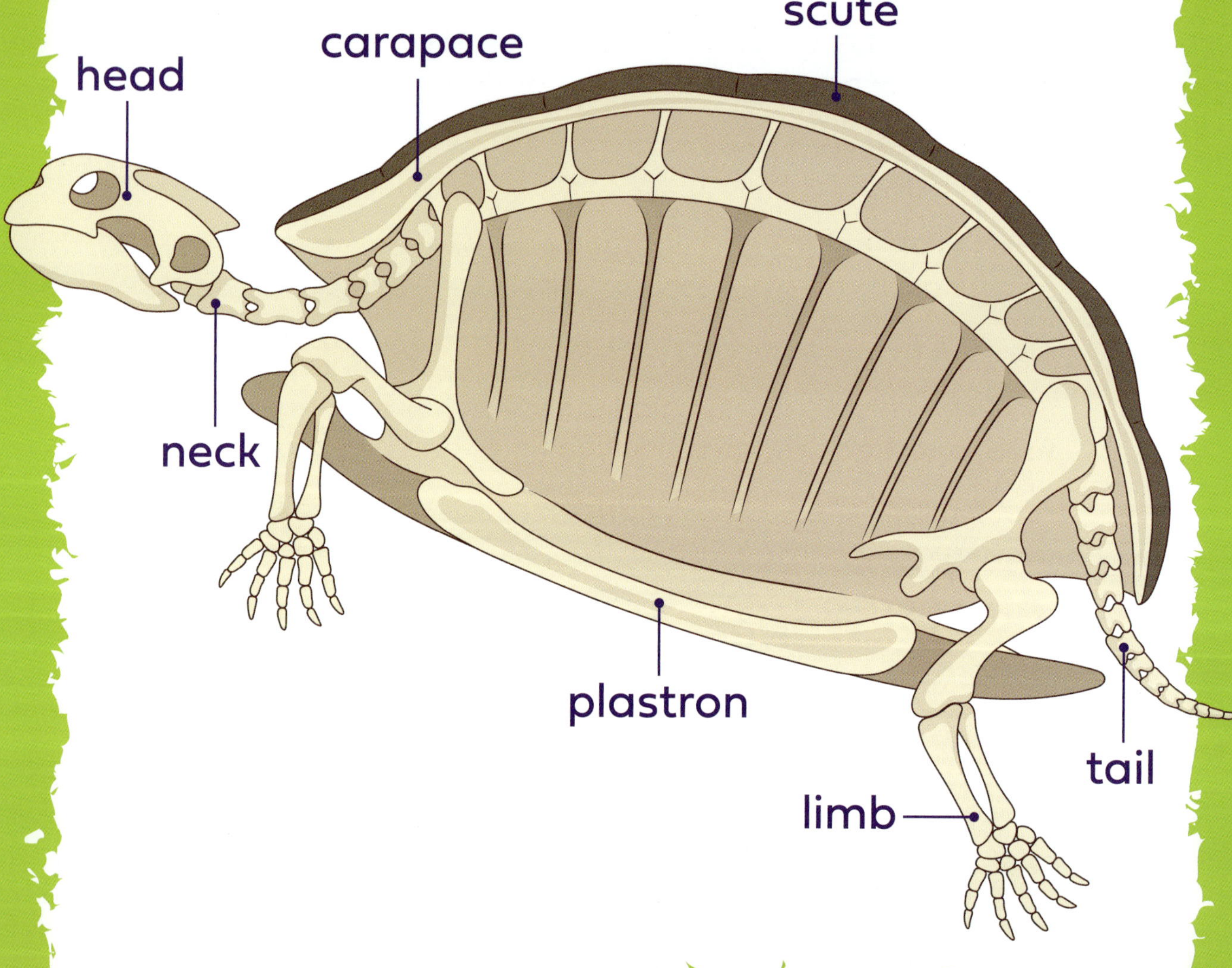

GLOSSARY

buoyant (BOI-uhnt) able to float

carapace (KER-uh-pase) a case or shield covering the back part of an animal such as a turtle

keratin (KER-uh-tin) a protein found in skin, hair, nails, turtle shells, and other body parts

organs (OR-guhnz) parts of the body, such as the heart and lungs, that have specific purposes

plastron (PLA-struhn) the bottom part of a turtle shell

predators (PRED-uh-turz) animals that hunt animals for food; a turtle's predators include foxes and alligators

reptile (REP-tile) a cold-blooded animal that usually reproduces by laying eggs

retract (ri-TRAKT) to draw back or pull in

scutes (scoots) hard, bony plates or scales that cover and protect a turtle or other reptile

tortoise (TOR-tuhs) a turtle that lives only on land and eats only plants

FURTHER READING

Montgomery, Sy. *The Book of Turtles.* Clarion Books, 2023.

Somaweera, Ruchira. *The Ultimate Book of Reptiles.* National Geographic Kids, 2023.

ON THE INTERNET

National Geographic Kids: 10 Totally Awesome Facts about Turtles!
natgeokids.com/uk/discover/animals/sea-life/turtle-facts
Learn amazing turtle facts.

Tennessee Aquarium: What Is a Turtle's Shell Made Of?
youtube.com/watch?v=glyXu55tis8
Learn all about turtle shells from a herpetologist at the aquarium.

The Parklands: DIY Turtle Shell
youtube.com/watch?v=S9bmMkyGL7k
Use art supplies to make your own turtle shell.

INDEX